BURN THE WITCH

poems by

Aïcha Martine Thiam

Finishing Line Press
Georgetown, Kentucky

BURN THE WITCH

poems by

Aïcha Martine Thiam

Finishing Line Press
Georgetown, Kentucky

BURN THE WITCH

Publisher: Leah Huete de Maines
Editor: Christen Kincaid
Cover Art: Elin Creese
Author Photo: Aïcha Martine Thiam
Cover Design: Elizabeth Maines McCleavy

Order online: www.finishinglinepress.com
              also available on amazon.com

Author inquiries and mail orders:
Finishing Line Press
P. O. Box 1626
Georgetown, Kentucky 40324
U. S. A.

Table of Contents

III. I HOPE MY HEART FOLLOWS

I. GOOD WATER

Lady Macbeth

You sit atop a quaking earth
Sometimes you feel, when you lay your hand on the bed's surface
Tiny tremors running up its length

Perhaps they are the scores
Of all the gushing evils it saw you do here
Words and sighs like the aftershock of surprise

Put this in your mouth and hold it:
You were too young for the lessons you learned
But you would have learned them anyway

Woman, a Universe unto herself
Pyre onto which they threw every little thing that hurt
And every other thing that counted

Imagine yourself a poem, a running metaphor
Volta, life swiveled and whorled by guilt
The sound it makes is a seething kind of noise

People godding you while they tether you with one hand
Want more than you are being told you can get
Head scarred from all the glass ceilings you knocked into

It hurts, it is a yearning in which
One can never settle, because the other side of yearning
It comes at your heels, savage, thankless, tripping

Imagine yourself midway through the air
Trapeze flying as you discover that you are the dreaded Void
And you let go

Matryoshka-like, you trick: you are not kind
Kindness has sidestepped you, maybe this feeling shall pass
Crow-like over you, and swoop

Imagine feeling powerful and power-less
All at the same time. Imagine wanting to massacre, to maul
And being relegated as Grace and Mercy's figurehead

You sometimes wonder about the strain it takes to dangle-swing
Your hands they were always too small
Your fingers dry and twig-like

So you've decided to cross bridges
When you get to them
You are nobody's mother
You resent being vaunted as such
Away with their terrible glory, then

I'm going back to my crows, my martlets
My good water
And whatever comes from it

A Case Against Your Generous Insistence
on Inviting Me to Things

Tugging on the rocked imposter's boat and asking for that
lil bit of extra room inside, it's the stuff of exhaustion
dreams and collapses. Your people will playact and they'll
oblige and they'll xray and dissever me as soon as I turn.
Even the cat will sense the weirdness vibes and maroon me
with his coolness. I am not a crown glass frame. I can't
afford any more singes at the back of my head where my eyes
are. They'll dance around the no-no zone all evening, asking
with the absence of the actual ask-ing: why my forkbites
look the way they do why I grip the knife too hard why I
swirl the deadweight food around. And you, by benevolent
deflection, will only center said no-no even more. Yes,
you mean well. Most days I think I do, too. But your kindness
is trouble wrapped in trouble. And though you'd never voice
it: at this point, your weariness, matching only mine, will
be apparent in the hemic tint of your fingertips tapping
fingertips. Next we'll move on to films and this'll really be
it. I'll say you guys choose. You'll insist, say I'm the special
occasion, singling out with that word—occasion—my foreign-ness.
And you and yours will morphose into a flock of restless parrots:
I thought you liked this one, I thought you liked this one.
But every choice will be thin ice: cinephile, yes, but faced
with minefield options. This one on fashion might mention
bodies, mention weight. This tragicomedy will make of trauma
a diluted joke. This documentary will confront your people
with their white privilege (and though I do this dance on the
regular, with you watching, fussing, fretful, it'll hit
very different). So I'll settle on something stupid we'll all
hate, but that won't hate us back in kind. And every time I'll
go outside to thread up some composure, you'll feel you have
to, casual, follow. We'll ogle the distance between your
balcony and the concrete underneath. We'll ha-ha and temper
the nasty inside joke

you: no funny business!
me: wasn't thinking about it!

And calling it a night, though early, will feel both a
deliverance, and
a defeat.

You love me, but I ruin things. Let's not like each other less.

sinker

the sound my clavicle makes when i rattle on it is tympanic
blue note
minor seventh dissonance
bone of my finger hiccups
over grooves and depressions of the sternum
disappear
some days i'm afraid i will disappear
the top of my nail curves forward
at a sharp angle
one i always forget to sand over
every bone in my body rings a ditty
learned by muscle memory
good luck with the earworm
the index is made up of the
distal
middle
proximal phalanxes
plus that index metacarpal
i play chopsticks on my thoracic vertebrae
invoke chopin like euterpe
the scales i practice on myself
the scale on which i step and bargain
somewhere in there there's a punchline
and octaves of irony
i want my fingers to tickle
trill-trill
the deep part of my throat
i want to push and taste
everything i guzzled while i sang
i want my skin to hug
the contours of my bones ever faithfully
i am faithful to my shrinkage
emily grierson to her desiccated corpse lover
except both emily and the lover are myself
except i have no love for myself
tritone dissonance reminds
that i bartered that one for a sense

of belonging
for oneness with that hunger
that sits right near my jugular notch

Apples, Oranges

I look up words I don't know;
in that breath of a moment between the curiousness
and the revelation,
I rediscover forgotten things:
                              the waiting
                              the zesty trepidation
                              the pleasure rush
                              that thistly 'looking forward to things'
misplaced so long ago.

"Jejune" distracted from a ripping headache
during which I considered
a hot iron pressed to my windpipe so as to
sear that which was attempting to claw its way
out.
By the time I learned it meant "simplistic,"
like an exhale:
the searing itch had passed.

Was reading up on staving off manic phases,
phone at a parallel angle to my face,
when out of torpor I jumped at "atavistic."
This is new.
Hadn't said that about a thing in years;
turns out it simply meant "ancient,"
the exoticism of the word a pretty charmer
next to its less impressive definition.

Similarly with "fulcrum,"
which isn't as interesting as it sounds.
Still, for those few seconds,
I held a palm right up to
the panic attack's prying face.
I almost even laughed,
struck by its similarity
to 'fous le camp'.

Pudendum.
Stalwart.
Gainsay.
Hosta.
Don't make me sound smarter than I think I am;
I've been warned about sounding pretentious,
dictionaries a time bomb in my green hands.

Senescence.
Knoll.
Winnow.
Gladioli.
Words in truth as simple refuge,
but nobody gives a shit about all the
litterature comparée I do in my head.

When I misplace Meaning and Sanity's strands,
I'd grasp for anything that imbues
the sprinting seconds with some sparkle,
an analogy for everything else,
one so lazy I dare only to write it down.

Sometimes I realize I was looking up a word I already knew;
those disappointments are worse than the comedown of figuring out
something
I actually did *not* know.

This Is Not a Complicated Memory

Although she queries mercy everywhere,
she likes playing with fire, she knows
that about herself. So when she asks
—for a friend—what, *exactly,* is the
definition of assault, she challenges
every explanation offered her and emerges
vindicated. See? For her (friend), it was
much more grey zone, and it was ages ago,
and he wasn't a stranger, and what he did—
anyway.
                Couldn't be.
Wasn't it.
                Moving on.

When she hears of people dying, she forgets
to say sorry before she asks how it happened.
Or in truth, the forgetting is intentional.
Why not spare a thought for the departed
before comforting the dispossessed? Another
orphic form of mercy. To look ahead, and
outward, when behind and closer to home—
anyway.

In her most vivid dream, a Lac Rose Lébou
told her she was an island. But not in the
"no man is" way, in the actual sense of the
word, land button-dropped in middle of water,
way. Smoothing the sea around her like her
very own teal blanket, spying on the moon's
two-step above, until its count, too, loses her:
it's no wonder she's mixing her decades and
her centuries. She thought she'd grow out of it
along with the heights, but her inches are slow,
and slow she stayed wanting. The risingsetting
sun carves grooves into the sky, and she sits
swaying above her body and loathing all of it,
and all it could not help her fend off;
accosting, questioning, how it came to be that...
but anyway.

Future Self Will Thank You For This

i.

When I was nine I went chasing phosphorescent cowrie shells in the seabed of my aunt's beach. My cousins' laughter like cooing seagulls, their waltzing shadows backdropped ways away. I became prescient, I pre-tasted things to come. I swam under the West African sun, ablaze, and I was 18 years from now, 27, though I didn't know it at the time. Remember: I was prescient, contemplating the weight of words, all of the words ever, ones I wrote and ones I felt around for, endless, what a stream. Before I knew it: the playful, scavenging waves mistook me for a spore of seaweed, ladled my little girl body up, around. I pinwheeled, I gyred, I moved back and forward in time, I drank tides,

I thought: something monumental is happening.
I thought: I am drowning.

ii.

I want to talk about the orgasm of death for a jiff a tired diluted analogy but at last years before I would understand what it meant I understood what it meant right before the paroxysm bubbled breath offered like a soggy gift I tasted cherries I climaxed Dutch acts in sea of Dakar a sleep cure for the ages what more fitting than to die where your ancestors lived what more fitting than to drown in the waters from whence you came these things they come in threes this is what I said what I want to say what I heard instead

iii.

Write this down. If you get
out of this, put it into words,
weave those sentences. Later,
when you will have exhausted
the thought of The End, breathed
it, seen it eyes closed,
fantasized all the dancing you'd
do together; later, when you
almost palm one pill too many
or dig that blade a little too
deep, toe the edges of curbs
and hope for winds to do what
your recklessness will not;

when you stop just. short.
enough. it will be good to
remember how it tasted,
how glorious, how freeing,
how promising. You will
remember the cherries, the
pinwheeling weightlessness,
and you will know that coming
home is just a cowrie's chase
and a playful wave away.

This Would Ruin My Life

O would call me Mélanie, between battement tendus, when
        signaling to correct my posture (even though I'd long

begged for Aïcha, and even later, relenting, settled
        for Martine). The misnaming would be chased by affable

self-chastisement. *Oh, je m'excuse! you look like a Mélanie*
        I know, can't seem to divorce you in my head.

And (smothering the other retort: *why, exactly, do I look*
        like that Mélanie?) I would beam right back. No worries

O, I know how things can get, MélanieMartineMélanie,
        it's like a phonic thaumatrope for the best of us.

And I loved O, doubly: first in instance-slices between
        detesting how her unyielding teachings revealed me my

body's limitations, because she sometimes revealed it to
        me beautiful. And then, in ripples of gratitude,

her flawed offer of my doppelgänger, an out: who was this
        Mélanie, and could I be her? And could I let her

step into my life and let me retire from it, I the
        hornworm and Mélanie, the braconid wasp gnawing

at my softest edges? And could I look at that sleety
        studio mirror every day and dissect the stranger

therein, with the funhouse mirror physique, knowing she
        was not me, not ever me? And could I uncage the

vicious bird in my chest, snug with the knowledge that it
        was Mélanie's, not mine, undoing my loved ones with its

assailings? I knew: *not Mélanie, Aïcha Martine, when you*
        say it, say it with your chest was something I

couldn't yet ask. I knew: at this point, if she called me
        by my name—by *my* name? it would ruin my life.

Once, O told me, while balancing it in her palm, how elegant
        she thought my thigh was, knowing not how

much I needed to hear that when I did, bent over sinks as I was
        eight times a day, trying to chisel them off.

And she could be tender in her chastisements; and really,
        I knew how things could get when one taught so many,

and so often; and MélanieMartineMélanieMartine,
        who wouldn't confuse them both?

But let's be real.
That is not the reason why.
I overcorrect the memory;
my fouettés were always
too enthused.

One day I ran into the fabled Mélanie in the studio
        hallways and each knew who the other one was;

and not least because—at last—our skin tones recognized a
        kin, in an expanse of such paler ones:

because we saw, mirrored, the same weary question, which
        neither of us bothered to ask. *Why?*

She doesn't even look like me. But isn't the trade nice,
        in a world that shuns you, as much as you shun yourself?

When You Let Me Come Up

I go straight for the bookshelves (capital offense if no books
present). I need to know what kind of crazy I am dealing with—

assuming, yes, that I am dealing with precisely that. You have,
after all, befriended me. You must know that you are doomed,

and not care, and I hate to break it to you, but—I digress.
I can't discern much about you from the Classics; your French

philosophers tell me nothing other than that we shared a Blaise Pascal
phase—don't all pretentious teenagers, at some point? Done that,

done that, read that. The *Russian Tales* are inspired: but some
people make the time for anger and anger doesn't seem like a

predilection of yours. I am rambling. *A History of the Black and
Tan Club*? An illustrated Kirikou novel? Ha. You've caught me for a

minute. I don't know what that says, but it says something and I am
listening. A sucker for ambiguity, I am. Genius and mundane, when

coin-tossed, often look the same. But I don't voice that. I cast a
much less vulnerable comment over my shoulder at you, and your smile

pingpongs from your eyes to your lips and back. I'm one to talk.
I have far too many books about people dying, being dead, killing

themselves, barely surviving. I nervous laugh when asked for
recommendations. *What is the last thing you read?*, translated,

sounds like *tell me about your deepest, most unrelenting anguish.*
And though you've let me come up, it'll always be too soon for

that
kind
of
talk.

Tiny Joy

It happened one day, as you were walking down Wabash Avenue,
fresh from Montréal, that careless woman who'd broken your heart
a little more each year. You sometimes blame that city

but if you were honest with yourself, you would admit
it wasn't her, it was the weight of what you expected
she could fix. Nobody could fix that—again, if you were

being honest, which is not likely in this lifetime.
It happened, then, as you were exploring your new lover,
inhaling the windswept novelty of Chicago.

A new place in a country you hadn't returned to in years.
Easy to forget how you'd escaped with taunting words over your shoulder
like you'd done to city after city after city,

whacking pleading hands and cajoling vows aside:
you have seen the last of me, you ungrateful witch
(though you had thrown the offense and picked at the scab

with restless fingers until you were once again an outsider).
When you torrented out of Montréal, you vaulted over your old flame Maryland
and skedaddled straight West until Lake Michigan caught you

with a wink and a come-hither finger.
It happened, then, as you sauntered down Wabash Avenue
—and I am not stalling: but you see,

this thing, it was monumental in its smallness,
next to those other too-colossal things,
and I've been trying to put it into words—:

the petalled city, it slowly effloresced around you.
A person smiled, another nodded, a third one opened a door.
The sound of water harmonized with corner store jazz: you eased.

Hadn't felt that in too long, eyes always trained
inward or down as you saunter down streets
because being a walking woman, it is hard, being a Black one harder,

depending on where you are casting the die. Chicago grinned slowly, beckoned:
and you went. And not that you stayed infatuated for long,
and not that things have changed overnight, and your city-loves are less scary,

and not that you will ever understand the concept of home,
and not that this country hates you any less.
But you always wait for the sign, the one that says, even for a second:

come closer, let's dance, try and see if you can keep up.
You were Seen. It was nice. Sometimes, you just want
to write something down because it is nice.

A Little Relaxer

We get skittish
when we are called
'pretty'. We wait for
the trusty appendix,
like a *tap* on the
angry skull: for a
Black girl. Matter
of fact, we get
skittish for nothing
at all, *tap tap*
sounds to the feel
of prickly panic
on our heads. A
little relaxer in
the form of addendums
all your life will
do it to you. *Tap*
alerts the dormant
thing on your scalp,
that secret language
all us melanated
girls yield via
sucking-air teeth
and screwed *get*
this off me eyes.
The things we do
we're told, the
things we're taught
will make us look,
be good. A little
relaxer of a life
is what we've long
earned. A little
relax her, give
her what she
deserves with a
good for you and a

tap on the backhead
to boot. We get
skittish when we
are called 'pretty'.
Tap comes like a
Just-For-Me pinprick,
the cajolery like
everything else in
life: open-ended,
waiting on the
shadow burn to
feel replete.

THIS IS MANIA

every time i see you again, after it's been a while,
i get into my bullshit song and dance. this being about
circling the same avenues, but never leaving them behind;
this being about losing ourselves in faraway affirmations.

punctuating the insincerity of it all, we banter.
do you still believe in ghosts? i laugh: do i
look like that kind of person (although i am)?
every time i see you again, after it's been a while,

for a mischievous minute, we are glorious again.
time is an eraser, failure is a hater's lie; we could
chew the fat all night: i am briefly reminded of why,
every time i see you again, after it's been a while.

woman, you are something else. merry skeletons
should not lie in bed like so. your osseous finger draws
me in, pressing, carnal. i should never romanticize: but
every time i see you again, after it's been a while,

i feel like you have spun me up from gold, made me up
of twine that dolls me up real good: i am compelling again—
until it catches on barbs, mangles me on my way down.
every time i see you again, after it's been a while:

this being about looking into far-flung lights and seeing nothing,
this being about second chances and course corrections,
this being about lighting matches against others, selflessness,
every time i see you again. after it's been a while,

i recall why i favored that other, denser sorrow, who at least lets
me sleep. i write myself meaner than i am. i suck on lies like
tongue candies. i throw away the words that don't make sense.
i snuff out the offbeat fantasies i don't subscribe to without you.

my week off

i ask for the room by the window

they say honey, you know this isn't a hotel, right?
but kindly, like i just don't understand things yet

i heard doctors don't have a sense of humor, that if they
do, it is phonecord extra-twisted

so i don't ask about the "cleaning fee" and the "checkout
early" discount
or quip "i'll send you a postcard when i'm out"

in fact i know not to ask for much
i'm supposed to revel in the multiverses they show me
and promise never to scoff at tenderness again

i know the drill

when you are tired, people love to slip in their two cents, unaware that there is
tired, and then there is tired-tired, and the intervals between them are farcical

inspirational drivel tells me
don't be afraid! go your own way! find your dazzled path! hold fast the adventure!

dangerous advice for a girl like me with a foot out the
door and any excuse to bail on her lantern dreams and
aspirations

no matter.

i have decided to swallow cyclones again and flick albatrosses off my shoulders
            get giddy around bedtime
            eat like i am three years old again
            read until my marbles fall out
            practice laughing like my chest is harmonica

when the nurse gets leery-eyed at this epicurean development in the story, i echo my people's helpful feedback:

girl, stop worrying. you need to take a vacation!

Prenostalgic Aphorisms

I'm so thankful for the conditional tense:
it could be worse is less tongue-acerbic
than *everyday for you is the Hour of Lead.*

I'd have been another strange fruit on my
country's strangest tree, I'd have fistfought
the Storm everyday with the knowledge that

nobody would give a lashbat if I died. I'd
have dressed up my wounds with precepts;
yesterday, tomorrow, but never today.

I'm so thankful for the bullets I dodged,
for the many times I
>   almost, but didn't completely—
>   stopped just short of—
>   could as well have—
>   and also, well-nigh—

But conditional bullet talk, it feels appropriated,
it is on the nose, it is teasing irony itself.
It has shown me my mortality greater than

that other subtle, everyday death, than the
reality of a trigger-happy (well no, not happy,
rankled) existence ever could.

The Forest, Not the Trees

I am prowling for inspiration again
Camels can go weeks without eating
I prefer the olm's tenacity (ten years!)
One is sad because I remind her of sadness

Camels can go weeks without eating
One says get better: I throw that up with the rest
One is sad because I remind her of sadness
I don't know if this is true but also, it is true

One says get better: vomit that supplication with the rest
Oyster, I am the world, this is just another alchemy
I don't know if this is true but also, it is true
One year off your life for the body you want

Oyster, I am the world and this is just another alchemy
Brittle bones, overt disgrace for the body you want
One year off your life for the body you want
Neither fish nor fowl. I am hungry: am I smiling?

(It's Because) I'm a Maximalist

I don't recall.
Did it always
sink and bloom
this way? Funny.
What was I looking
at all those times
distorted, spent
microdissecting?
Surely not phases,
phases teach small,
Subtle Things, and
me? Maximalist at
the jazzy core.
Listen, but don't
too hard. If I knew
what shape my body
was, wouldn't know
what to barter for:
teacup breasts;
nail face smoothie;
slack-toothed sly;
iron iris eyes.
In a storm I'm a
good man, and also
the storm, and
that soft ensuing
letup, and the
bellow that precedes
and everything
I forgot to name:
Werewolf and the
Moon, Selkie
and the shedded
epidermis, the
crabapple, the seed,
the bitter left
on bluest tongues.

I clapped to
make the waves and
careened them over
at the stillness.
The squall it
kicked up in its
wake is how I knew
how
fast

        my
        body

                        could
                        fall.

Anything, Really

I never really paid attention to my grandmother's feet
Forgot exactly how the skin arches and molds around the toes
And those toes, what do they look like
I try to remember the shape and feel of her hands
I've been told mine look like hers, but cannot really be sure

I didn't watch when she'd take them into hers and press

That dry shock of a handshake, strong enough to knead the millet for the thiéré,
to deal sharp blows to the back of misbehaving little heads, to braid lush kinky
hair into soaring works of art

I think of doing those things too, but I cannot trust the hearsay and the
assurance of our likeness
So I do them timidly
Which is precisely who she was not
What did her eyes look, really look like
She has my father's, but there were nuances
Did he get her gap teeth from her too
I come close to forming a picture, never close enough

I don't know whether to be proud of my gait, the cadence of my sentences, the
roll of my tired shoulders, won't be, until and unless I know how deeply rooted
they are, and where

Which is to say I never might
I would have paid attention, but how could I know
How quickly the effigy
Would slip away before her time
I take pictures, lots of pictures
I draw with fevered hope
That I might seal my fingers around that silky water
Before it, too, uproots and washes her from me

Sidestage

Time passes differently here   you were envisioning trampolines   now you are
headed for concrete   sit on your hands   sit upright and don't get comfortable
never comfortable   who said a bird in the hand should have gone for a different
metaphor   the puss moth eats its own skin after it has shed it   now that is
cashing out and cashing in   sit your legs under you   sit apart   sit so they
don't see it when you slouch   you've landed in worse places   with agony and
its also-rans   so   sit so they can't see your face   see it wrinkle wishwashed in
fear   get yours   get yours all the way   sit so you still look woman and a threat
sit so the whole world knows   this here bitch has some power imminent   it's
a ten of pentacles kind of day   call yourself circe making out of pigs men   sit
like a trick   on the sideline   clothe yourself in others' shadows   you've
landed in worse places   you've been dragged into the light   singled out for
your atrocity   you said never again now you have to mean it   sit by the corner
let them take the stage center   sit so nimble they mistake you for decor   you
were headed for concrete   now you're back looking skyward   they see you
they see only washout misfire letdown   they list in order skin sex origin   they
say I don't think so   so get your shit together   you puss-moth, you   sit like
you're the last sentence   they'd have thought to string together   sit like they
won't even know   won't even know what hit them.

Congratulations! You're In A Cult

The last time someone asked how I was holding up, the visceral lie cut in line
to stunt on all the candid things I almost said. I've been known to prick holes
into the bottom of heart-heavy things. So take what I say with a grain of salt:
but I happen to know that batshit girls make the best friends in need.

It is true,
I have been them.

Behold:

my co-disciples and I, flagellating ourselves (for what again, I forget), heaving
self-deception turned sabulous truth, touting this magic made from carnage,
transcendence from sorrow.

The self-harmer will put a therapist to shame with her cut-through perspicacity.
   The suicide ideator will sell you life's momentousness to save your soul.
    The bulimic offers ipecac like it's water after a sun-soaked day.

An upper for the landfall,

          a sip,

            a tip,

              a nudge.

Behold:

our toothpick knees frayed in supplication, lint in eyes, hair in mouths, going
        I got this I got this yeah yeah I got this

Even you'd idle and watch the trainwreck.

Maybe this is the reformed disciple in me, conjuring up a softer, stand-in reality;
maybe it's my third eye talking, persuaded it sees clearer than the other two;
maybe I went looking for home again, and pro-ana houses seemed like solid
talus caves;
do not judge me, I know better now: this wisdom, it takes work.

But then again the last time someone asked to shoulder the space under my paperweight heart, I Irish Goodbye-d out of there like a thief on fire.
So (I'm not exactly a reliable source) take what I say
with a grain of salt.

Trick of the Light

When I was 17 I leaned my forehead against the dirty window of a bus
and made a promise to the going-to-bed-now sun: this time would be the last.
And for many years (3 and a half to be specific) that promise was protected.
I never severed: you see? I don't always lie, I don't always say things
just to say things. Water, she harbors her own light. I was made to believe

in something mutable, shapeless, not in the truth. These fictions carry
so much within their sodden folds, they find themselves submerged,
drenched, and I drink and drink and I drink every time. When I was seventeen
I became a teetotaler. When I was seventeen, saw more clearly than probably
ever would again. How many times have I seen it, that other water I partook of

more than once? Wanda Coleman unmasked Saturday Afternoon as the killer.
Mine was always that acerbic Friday Morning, cusp day, when old things
are passing on over, new ones pledged to begin, and I stay rooted
in the hour, straight razor in the hand, deciding, deciding.
How many times have I seen my own blood? Put that bad water down.

Nobody will know that you are gone, not that you reach on back anyway,
not that you look away from madness' lighthouse enough to make
your screaming self heard. How many times have you seen your own blood?
Reverse-engineered creation with each slit-hacking and sawing?
What happened when you were 17? Why not now? Hark! Here is a child

who thinks she knows everything. Here is a child who has never learned
to count, even when all cards were in her hands, a flush. Been parading
marked skin for years before in-denial eyes, in front of can't-answer-now
tongues, of ask-again-tomorrow pouts. So this is me asking now,
Richie Tenenbaum over a sink: how many times, how many times now?

I don't always lie, but I seldom tell the truth at the urgent, vital hour.
There is an explanation in that deciding. Too many questions. I can't
say it now. Later though, I promise—yes, promise—to tell you.

II. MOON WHISTLE

grapevine gossip

from time to time i look up a man i almost
dated to test my intuition's mettle
the addendums i append to my search
varying only in their extremity

      firstlast   *+ jail*
                                  + serial killer
                                  + murder

can't help but probe, set stiff set stiff
for the soft spot in my duodenum where
my foresight rests, and try to prove
it wrong, and my other senses too

that my bloodhound ears didn't register
what they think they registered while he
was threading me metal spools of sparkling
ovations, so sharp they gashed when handled

all that talk of redemption, all that
tell me what scares you, for i am scared too
trifectas the two-pronged truth, my beast
recognizes in him a wholly deeper beast

softspot screams the very first song i, newborn
woman, heard offered me: *runrunrun for the hills*
can't help but silence it, set stiff set stiff
or maybe it's admission to that club i'm

rescinding, the one that standardizes
ambidextrous horror—*we've all dated a creep*—
until it, too, internalized, feels like a dinky
pinch, duodenum subdued to ruination

from time to time i google a man i almost dated
and am stunned to learn he hasn't killed anyone
                                yet

and though i am momentarily comforted, assurance in
others' inner workings set stiff set stiff
my softspot-foresight promises, wasn't *all in your head, you just wait, you just wait.*

ON THAT GHOST WE SAW IN THE PARK IN POTOMAC

we lie under arched ceilings
of sugar
maple trees. was it dark, this
another
evening of fogs and shadows?
no, just me
dressing up plain-ish stories
as always.
was more near soft-like, golden,
and mothers
chasing somber mood-clouds have
sent us off
to chase sleeveless errands in
turn. *go fetch*
—not a word from you now, go—
that salmon
shaped plate i left in the park.
and though we
take it to mean a pretext,
gretel-style
(because hansel gets killed in
the woods), we
roam forests for kitchen plates.
trees titter
incandescent, warm-yellow;
we turn loose;
we confetti fallen leaves
and pretend
they're bowls tossed at adult heads;
curious fawns
look like friends we've never had.
why go back?
why not woods-house where we thrive
unfettered,
far from virulent mood-clouds?
one of us

(we still debate this), juiced up,
calls to her,
she who hangs about these ways:
we feel bold,
and shouldn't be. *she's just a*
hag, they say,
and ghosts, they don't come when called.
but she does.
heard you looking for a plate?
as a kid,
i went chasing mine, and just
kept walking.
she is no hammer horror
character,
no sea-colored hotel ghost;
in fact she
more than looks like us. seconds
before we
take off sprinting, yowling, back
to mothers
we are gifted wisdom pearls
from her words
though we won't know it just yet.
even if
you wander willingly in
to the woods,
always palm your breadcrumbs.
my friend now
lives on the neutral side of
misery.
i cherish my innermost
hauntings, and
walk into rooms without a
plan, and my
mother and i still haven't
found that plate.

Esprit d'Escalier

Z, picture us in your
    tiled sea-foam green
        bathroom. Ticking off,

           like so, the little box for
      "COMPARING NAKED
BODIES" in the book of

Female Intimacy Initiatory
    Rites. You rumbled loudly
      you are so lucky, my

        skin dissents, couldn't
    swallow my bruises'
  stains like yours does. I

wish I could bleed in
    secret, I wish I could.
      Oh, scratch that. We were

        12 year old birdbrains,
    we never spoke with
  such sophistication.

But the gist of it was
    nearby, that day. You
      were going to have it

        hard in life, and I
    might, but at least it
wouldn't show. You went

see, this right here.
    Yesterday I bit your
      forearm and it doesn't

come. And I tough-gal
swaggered around the room
chanting 'nobody asks me

what is wrong' like I'd
been wishbone-favored.
You almost sold me on

the dream, Z; only you
could do that under the
glossy pretense that you

loved me so much, which
must mean that you knew
and saw me best. You

looked at me desiring
yourself, and I took in
your areolae, the color

of my favorite Starburst,
thinking mine (already
deflated in anticipation

of the years to come) were
a bit more like sea-weed
flaked around its fringes.

Sometimes when, idle,
I pinch my chilly teat,
I get the taste of candy,

tart but sweet, and my
gums water. I wonder, when
you think of sea-weed, if

your mouth puckers too.
I haven't summoned eyes
and the ensuing candor

in heaven knows x many
years. Nowadays: I've
taken to brutal snubbing

of Commiseration. When
women want to bare to me
I say 'this ain't the

Pain Olympics' and carry
on. Nowadays: I say 'don't
dare ask me what is wrong'.

Though we were discussing
different kinds of bruises
then, though I still love

the dream you sold me, 'you
are so lucky' shreds my guts
every day. It's been universes

since. Wherever you are,
allow me this one pettiness,
Z:

you
were
wrong.

Pleasure Sounds

You're gonna have to give me a minute: I'm trying to knock back the last
  dredges of sleep
That time/space juncture when I talk too much, my brain a loosened enclave
A deviated stream of feather-light speech, of smoldered sounds and moans
My mouth is blue, my words are crimson, lace shame up like boot along
  glittering leg

That time/space juncture when I talk too much, my brain a loosened enclave
Whispered in tongues at the cost of my lungs: but what are lungs if not truth
  instruments
My mouth is blue, my words are crimson, lace shame up like boot along
  glittering leg
Utters: I wish you called less I wish harm would continue interfering

Whispered in tongues at the cost of lungs: but what are lungs if not a truth
  instrument
Says: with every phone call I hope for calamity, but settle for disquiet
Utters: I wish you visited less I wish harm would continue interloping
And that: I peak when people bruise me, I don't know how to love

Says: with every phone call I hope for calamity, but settle for disquiet
Says: yes, touch me there and leave. This can be the end, this sounds like a
  song.
Says: I peak when people bruise me, that I do not want the love
When I sleep well, I will tell you, peacock feathers graze-grazing up the length
  of me.

Blood Magic

i.

When we fight, skin tender from a petty blow,
scalp sore from a fistful of braids pulled solid,
afterwards, we cut up white tissues into bitbitbits and
swallow, conjure we have made our own, drawing the world around us
in our own lovely image. Apology, casual and clear, hinges on
the sacraments we make, us being eight and ten and thirteen and fourteen.
Finger pricking finger, blood to blood, seals a promise or a lie,
sometimes a crooked pact at least one of us will pretend to forget years on.
Cap ou pas cap, I'm rubber you're glue, qui va à la chasse perd sa place and
　　whatnot:
we aren't adults, crying wolves, squandering tolerance and compassion.
When my lifeblood spills into yours it sings music-like,
water returned to water, form gone back to form.
When our essence collides, it shakes and rattles the world, rubble cast to feet.
Sight to behold, terrible only to those who don't know
what it is to carry another person within you,
to hate and love as forcefully as if, in fact
it were not at them, but at your very own self.
Prismatic, dizzying in its divinity,
song and dance tests your mettle and takes
everything from you—but still it dares you *keep playing,*
even in the pointless hour, even in the thankless one.
We proffer white tissues as if to sop up all of it unspilt,
that which binds us flesh to soul.
The slight forgotten, the injury dull-dulled, the barbed word
still latching but easier to pluck out.
Borrowed comb, torn skirt, stinging insult, spiteful lie:
who am I trying to forgive?

ii.

One day she sees someone shred a stark-white tissue,
seated on the table beside them. A child;
and she almost leaves the Today moment and the tenseness therein,
the emotion being shattered in the negative space between them,

this replica of an exchange she has had with infinite people,
almost lovers, suddenly friends, broken strangers, even herself.
She has lost the facile compassion, that curiosity for crooked pacts.
Who am I trying to forgive is a misshapen song;
keep playing, pointless, thankless as ever.
But who are you, quiet one, without your kin,
the only place you could call home?
Now that is the question: no wonder she is lost.
The Leaving, it lasts a violent second and they intrude:
the negative space the forlorn child the shredding of the white tissues.
She looks past the man and sees others before her, and she can only watch,
and the concerto of rrrrrripping, it baits her memories.
Wishing peace could be conjured and achieved so easily,
she knows no amount of wanting, no amount of magical thinking,
no amount of talking will mend what has happened here,
has been happening for rising, then crashing years.
Which reminds her: she hasn't spoken to her brother in a few weeks,
has lost sight of two sisters, in bursts, and then a long, tracking shot,
and her other sibling's words lie idle in her phone.
The adults crying wolves have had their say, not in form of howls,
but a sulk that makes cut up tissues pointless.
Why remedy to that which has not been felt/seen/said in years?

You Were Sleeping So Well

You don't remember the first time you saw, really saw the
chroma of your skin; but you remember what it felt like to
want to rub its sootiness from the canvas underneath. The day
those planes collided in New York, and they pulled all of you
wailing out of school, you knew the giddy games were over.
Not Christian + White = not from here after all. You were
sleeping so well, courting post-Y2K frenzybliss, the thrill
of technophobia a barometer, what formidable days to come.
Even when lost on you, back then, you joined all choruses:
all hail Sean and Shawn, the Napster kings! You yourself,
queen of your microcosm, you were not somewhere you came
from. You were one of 6 billion, and Pluto was a planet, and
"them" meant anyone, but never you. You don't remember
the texture of its symmetry, you don't remember how the
world, holding itself together by the tension of something
promising, brought you to your feet slanted. Beautiful torpor
era, vantage point romances, 90s girl buying into the myth
of safety, shut-eyed through the night; though you were
sleeping so well you didn't realize the myth, they weren't
selling it to kids who looked like you. Even when that boy in
maternelle called you NEGRO, even when speaking anything
but English to your mother attracted buzzing glares in public,
even when the nice ones asked did you come by boat and from a
hut, you were sleeping so well the ugliness, split through its
pulpous middle, looked peripheral, hazy, unfocused. A concept,
like the death of grunge. You were sleeping so well you did
not realize everyone else had woken up, judging you the way
you would someone who'd been kicking in bed, disrupting
everything, although you, much later, would not remember what
you'd done. Suddenly you were goldfish in fishtank, no longer
salmon fighting upstream, or whatever the hell else they told
you as consolation for having been born Pisces. Suddenly they
showed you yourself and it was blasphemous to look away; and
"them" was you, and you were one, not 6 billion, and you were
where you came from, and the texture of the world matched its
jagged symmetry. You were sleeping so well as if you knew,
it would be heavy-lidded whiles before you slept right again.

unmoor

drag finger down the length of a known one's forearm like this morning, on dusty elevator wall. dust on finger tells a story, but skin on skin too seldom does. can't relate. you excite tumult when you do things like this, but won't stop you, never has before. can't relate, can't relate and need to.

palpate your mother's hair to find alikeness. steal a pat-pat from your father, casual and all. baby handed makes you recoil, but still, trace and trace the skin to seek it. what ties you to them, to anyone. can't relate. shun being touched, and need it like you need water. it will make it make sense.

wake when someone breaks from a hug before you're ready to. everything, everything. a palm on a door handled just swiveled by another palm. what does warmth mean. at this point, would say yes to anything you would.

when you touch, it is not closeness you hunt but what lurks underneath. significance, something like it. your eye finds another one's eye and you feel yourself. you come in focus and you feel yourself, chest contractions, tongue 'tween teeth, toe in searing sand but it blinks and gone again you are. can't relate, wish you could.

have forgotten how to comfort people. drag fingers down the length of things instead, hoping you will leave equivalent trace. burst into existence with pinching heart falling in love with everyone smiles your way but reel when a person touches you but tracing the outline of a forearm wishing it around you but sitting sideways and out on any chair it hurts it hurts. did this to yourself, will continue to.

when the car veers too much on the side and bodies melt sideways into bodies: for a moment you are one and the same. hip bones grind into each other, shoulders rub against, skin borrows another skin's softness-warmth. in this moment, closer kind of art than you have ever felt, made, known. will you continue casting spells until and until and until you can relate? you will.

# of tongues and flames and gratitude

in three years will be twenty since i
started spleening and letting tongues of
flame lick the length of me. in three years
will be ten since i gave that gorgeous
precipice the eye, wishing to fall,
and that minx flirted right back at me.
in three years eight since i double take-d
corners where i thought i saw devil and co.
calling me to come along and play,
and others, others. took my cobains,
my winehouses too seriously.
said i'd never make it to thirty;
but anything can happen 'tween years
and years. in three years might even have
put a rope around the voice said that
black girls are magic but you'll never
have that kind of magic, kind that make
melanin pop-pop, every angle,
make you float ether-like over all
your detractors, including yourself.
kind that make even the bigots cock
an eyebrow and say whoa there now that's
something to see. in three years will be
fifteen since i took hammer to toe
in throe of frenzy, pushed exacto
knife to throat, rubbed mentholatum in
symmetrical cuts just to say i
felt what was what. i tell people i
have birthmarks all over my body.
if hatred of self were beauty i
would never have cause to hate again.
damn, those were crazy years. put that far
behind me, though, peachy-keen. convinced
self and others i am fine; but look
closer, check my pillow, still: there be
teeth marks where i bite down when in it
i howl. yet anything can happen

'tween years and years. in three years i could
learn my blessed ancestral language.
gratitude it pays for everything.
say thank you thank youthankyouthankyou;
my mother knew to tongue it even
and especially when the swelling
years showed up to heckle, and every
woman before; so shall the next ones,
too. they let you tolerate the taste
of it, no idle words, no idle
song, until everything that follows,
even the bygone and coming time,
even three years (give or take) carries
the tang of it, gratitude and all.

when he asks you why you never
speak up in group therapy

you could say:
back in school, when you knew the answers you wouldn't give them for fear of
looking like a goody-two-shoes.
now you know not to give them, but the context—my has it changed.
who's the dandiest? who's the most disaffected? who would fail, and how, for
being the teacher's pet?

you choose instead all the longs of the short:
because, just because.

because it's bad enough that you are bare, bad enough that you feel raw, the
question—et tu?—a vivid klieg light on your injuries.

because you've been standing off with another quiet girl and you want to see
who yields.

because at your most irritable you think you all sound like judy/punch
marionettes, brawling like you're getting at something significant.

because stillness is your happy place and there's no non-prick way to say it.

because it means proving your cracks exist, deepest where they most revolt
you—knowing or not knowing the depths of *their* cracks, and if they own
them, and since when.

because you're going to have a disagreement, and earnestness will earn you
nothing.

(and what does it even mean, group therapy, therapy for who, what group? do
we all splinter the same, then? are we percentiles of a larger suffering? and why
should we filter distinctions through generalities? and why should we meet
each other halfway? and why should i busy with your questions when i have my
own, like: why is it too much to ask to be seen for my personal fury?)

because it doesn't matter, and rumination is wastefulness: hurts coming up,
hurts coming down.

because if you prove that last fact wrong, you'll have to reckon with what your lifelong misanthropy has robbed you of.

because you will say all the above and you'll be presented with two choices
    leave the room and feign vindication
    stew in post-outburst shame, knowing you look as childish as jim stark

    doing chickie runs to prove he is a man.

Otherwoman

I've become familiar
        with the tip of my shoes of late.
You look people in the eye,
        you get what you must be asking for
In the form of:
        blink-and-you-miss-it scorn
poker hot man-rage
        finger-dented bruises
witty, smutty slur
        say it nicer, that's a good girl
I ain't your brother
        ain't your friend
I ain't your lover
        I ain't your friend
all the above
        in miscellaneous order.
Whoever said
        humanity's arc
tilted toward kindness
        was in evidence not an
Otherwoman.

after a while all lakes look the same

i can't find my footing || here || where the soil is always moving || wavelength surfing || tried to make sense of the panorama of homes || gyrating color like a fan || needle never settling too long on one place || humid craving in Dakar and muted radiance in Maryland || smoky wetness in Gabon || beats away the plump soils of Naivasha || i hope i never sound thankless for the panorama || but i have angered restlessness || made wanderlust escapism's pretext || i can't find my footing || let me remain somewhere where i am seated back fully to backrest || not with foot pointed outward || fingers grasping wood || just in case || to steady a runner's stance || let me find it in myself to hold || the notion || without shame or fear || that turns to hollow swagger || the sound of my sickness is not given weight here || because it is a bird that awaits permission || to settle || home || and i have yet to deliver || i hang over blush-colored Lake Retba || and i compare it to Lake Michigan and Lake Potomac || although i haven't seen the one in years || and the other since i was three || after a while all lakes look the same || constance only in my hatred for the sun and my yearning for the violent sea and my resentment of those who would argue those dogmas with me || heartsick || homesick || both strangers || bitterly familiar all the same || when did i stop saying thank you || probably when i realized || that motion would never stop claiming me || the same that makes me wake in one place || heart asleep somewhere i've never been || it is not just a motion of the body || the body can settle || the soul-sickness || once it tastes of wildness || once it believes home can be found and made there || it never stops its sailing

Never Was Your Color

It was a mistake after all to make the kitchen brighter.
All colors are known to lie, to prettify themselves

for the occasion. I draw my knees up on the granite floor
and against the windowed glass and have conversations

with the peach-swiped yellow wallpaper. I feign honesty.
I am a woman who can talk about grief and write out

that watercolored sadness I always brush my toes in.
I swear: I am a woman who can look a curving road in

the eye and say I know where this is going, I am a woman,
I have been here before. I can hold it together, come up

against a freshly wallpapered kitchen. Can say: this was
a mistake, no, don't think wallpaper, don't think yellow,

don't think about that story, you know the one;
I am a woman who can say: no you are not like that

protagonist with her sad life and almost mean it. Things
come and go—time's a nagger, checking in occasionally

(you still there, then?), green tea mug gets cold in hand,
petrichor gives way to a seabreeze kind of smell,

light makes its mad-dash way across the room,
onetwothreefourfivesixseven o'clock, my outline shrinks

and flickers before me, for a few hours, I am a giant
in contrejour—but yellow walls and I, we go nowhere.

I am a woman who can hold it together hold it together
hold it together. I need to learn other things

with my hands that aren't picking and picking and
picking apart. I heard dying felt like a flash, a burst,

life bottlenecked into a last huzzah. Somebody told me
it's a bend in the road you should outpace before

it finds you unawares. I am lying. I know dying feels
like a flash, a burst, life bottlenecked,

and nobody told me this, I did. Anything, anything but
this slow exercise of a—where was this going?

It was a mistake to make the wallpaper yellow. Now
my hands are full of it, the allegorical mistake

laid out like an exclamation on my fingertips. I am
a woman who can look a curving, bending mind and say:

you know where this is going, go to bed, you can already
hear the roar, you've had too good a couple of weeks.

And yellow? like that damned story, will pull you apart.
Never was your color—next time go at least for red.

Peacock Insight

Saying goes, when you let people wound you, you are actually in control of the bruise, of the dispensing of it, of its frequency, of its consonance: another trick of the light.

Prudence says, self-deprecate before you become the joke: when it stops causing funnies, all you need think is *I'm sure God loves me*, and that splits the hair just right.

Slowrumor has it, in order for masochism to save you, you call it by a different name; never the thing, never the thing itself. This beastie, it answers to Opportunism.

And also: when your nail polish starts to chip, just as you're getting used to the furious tone of your fingers wearing it, better to tell yourself it's the look you were going for anyway.

And hyperbolize the ways in which your body has betrayed you,
    until they become your It Factors—*call me Cool Girl.*
        And aggrandize your immunity to awful things until
            gaped-mouth, they whisper in your wake 'that's the one, that's
                the chick who…' And learn to take the backhand of insults
                    in glorious stride, and walk into rooms with a
                        fighting foot, andandand…

A man once assaulted me
right in front of my
apartment. Grabbing
my waist for effect,
he said (before 'I know
where you live' and after
'there's no point in the
tussling'): 'I always liked
a girl with small tits'.
So I guess that for all
my self-loathing, one
man's trash and whatnot.
And not to compare my

Self with trash, and not
to imply he had claim to
even an itoa of earth
I stood on, but I guess
hatred seeded inward will
sprout outward down
the line.   How's that for insight.

Hecate's Wheel

Convinced it tasted of soot and salt,
time and again I tried to bite off
the ink-blot stain on my tongue,
responsible, surely, for tinging
everything I drank with its essence.
That is, until I understood. In Senegal:
we inkblot tongues are soothsayers.
Anything we say comes supposably true,
contrapasso dispelled indiscriminately.
Should a wordsmith like me be thirsting for
that kind of omnipotence? I hope
to be one of the good, really good ones;
but buzzing bees in my elastic throat, I
know I go both ways with words, have
only mouthfuls of cursepells to offer.
To blazes with intent: I thought I wanted love
to feel like something belonged to me.
Why did I say: *I know when my flaming*
lifeblood hits the floor and bursts
outward like ember petals, I'll be
incandescent, the epicenter of disaster,
too fierce for love, too good for love.
When said love deserted me, I spent a violent
year supine on the coal floor beseeching
Take it back, I take it back I take it back.
I think I am one of the good, really good souls,
but it never occurs to me to say good, and to
wish for good. I cannot plagiarize what I've
never known. At the suggestion of pandemonium,
my inkblot tongue comes alive.
I could kill this liar with a prayer.
Even when my malice maimed the cruelest
boy I knew, omnipotence like the
resounding crack of a whip—
                              Again!
                                  Again!
I was Doubting Thomas, if he were a woman who'd been

taught and taught to disbelieve. A maelstrom
thrashed in my palms, and I still underestimated
how fearsome, how formidable
I could be.

scapegrace

       always
when things get (… get what?)
i feel like i did as a child
hiding from grownups during
early morning travels
people asking *where is she* clenches
every nerve in my body
sends delicious ripples down my legs
it is how i know i liked being held
       after all
lightning-quick, too hard, never more than once
but where it counts, always where it counts

       always
i feel i am under a table
hearing someone ask where i am
snug under dust-covered tablecloths
sampling yellow play-doh
       always
finding comfort in the comfort of uncomfortable thought
i am missing from an emotional space
       always, always
someone is looking for me

i want to say: hold me where it counts, only where
       it counts
hold my bruised ankle up in place
my swollen fingers too
my bleeding tongue between my teeth
       always
i buckle
       all ways
when i see tables, no matter how small
i glide glide underneath and kiss the panic
full-on in the mouth
ghosts don't get anxious
i need to play the part

it's easy enough to live a life
just pick one and go
have you ever been lonely
have you ever tried hiding in a city
where everyone knows you
lay me down here and i'll show you
        and also: do you sleep?
fraternize with spaces   like   this
to make the words   breeeaaathe
like i haven't in years

when did you grow up
        gently, between cracks and apertures when you weren't looking
when did you find the time
        when do any of us?
put your tongue out
where the burn is
the fire you court can't hurt you

what on earth could anyone else want from me?

i learn to listen to what people say when i am not there
conversations lapped up from under mahogany tables
words struggling from behind closed doors
truths that won't come out while i am on hand

something happens when i leave the room
        always
it claims a magic i don't feel when my body holds
the space

phantom crabs

i was never one for hope; it's more that febrile gratitude i courted when i managed to just scot-free from things (*alhamdoulillah*); shed the notion of nation when i felt it strip me from the notion of home; but when america, again, folded its arms around white supremacy; suddenly i didn't mind my melange so much; in fact i gripped it; held it back like a cur; let me put it this way; people look and don't see further than the obvious (*alhamdoulillah*); and those conversations parch right then and there; the 'Martine' in my name? it's a distraction; my west african legacy? it barely registers; had they known one of the quoteunquote towelheads being lambasted after 9/11 was me; wouldn't have mattered i was a child; and also mourning for my country; let me put it this way; when you throw a dart with a bad aim; hoping to bullseye it; you don't bitch when you miss the mark; you think at least i didn't put someone's eye out; those families trading surnames; to sound less arabic; they needed more distraction; than they could peddle; and even then i saw awful sacrifice; for what it was; and even then i could not judge; let me put it this way; scapegoating; it changes like the tide; sometimes i am hapless; sometimes i say 'thank god'; sometimes small shields are a mercy; sometimes you duck focus too late; so i take comfort in the arpeggiated revolt; in the oneness that protesting offers; all of us incomers; harmonized under our outsider's badge; yet every now and then; a slur offered someone else; nonetheless looks me dead in the eye; snarls *gotcha; thought you could hide*; let me put it this way; you can always raise your voice; and pound the asphalt; and throw the bigot dumbfounded; off his little bitty horse; and do and do and do the work; (*alhamdoulillah*) you are buffeted; under one disguise and under others; but the guilt/gratitude/terror/whatever; it finds you; pinches you merciless; asks; *did you? did you do enough?*

Evil Eye

At the center, taunting silence, wintered spirit. The core, aloneness.
    There is power in a still waters kind of Existence. The Self

has universes of time upon which to unfold its corrective depths.
    There is power in still waters, there is power in the eye

that manifests starved reality. My mother speaks of lines I don't see
    on her face; I start instead to imagine them on my self.

Everything about disorder, I've gleaned from looking at women:
    she has a fertile mouth, she has smiling eyes;

my dead grandmother says: get my name out of your mouth, stop wringing its
    juices to justify everything. You are duplicity itself.

That, there, is a newborn who looks like me. Darklovely like I was.
    I look, I think: she is going to have such a great life. I

circle-jerk myself, ouroboros-style, with the epithets I love to tack
    onto others. Look at them, look at yourself,

you are going to have such a great life. If I say this enough I might manifest
    starved reality, writ large, caps lock and bold-type, aye.

Please excuse the spillage, my world was moon-gray when I told you
    I was done surviving. It's just: I don't always like myself,

and pretty words offer a smashing refuge. I want to chew on wads of
    guilt, and be seen as I am, fruitless mouth, unsmiling eye.

I want to hear once and for all: not the center, not the sum of all things.
    Want to hear: there is no power when still waters is a Self.

Want to hear: where did you go wrong? And have the answer, and not need
    others to know, there is much more to me than meets the I.

Echo Chamber Sweet-Talk

I've been trying to wear love on my chest
and say it with my chest, but well-wishers,
they harry. Good luck, merry this, I wish you
that and more, it wears out my tensile
strength. Forget Emily Grierson: I am Hannah
asking Eva if she ever loved me, days before
I catch flame and she plunges out a window
to save my life. Survival. But what's the point
of survival on the balance of a single foot,
half-masticated, barely swallowed, held by
slack and bitter fingertips, kept in bosom
barely sighing relief? Caution, meet Wind:
what's the point of survival in which cessation
is welcomed open-armed at turn and turn? In which
life is an onus blanket swathed and tucked
over perspiring bodies? Life looks after like,
we cannot see you waste it, so they say: but
what's the point of survival in which pinpricked
heart self-vandalizes at waxwaning breaks? Shall
I shoulder the posthumous guilt for giving the
go-by a second look? Where afterlife unfolds,
could my weightless shoulders do it then?
Right now a mother's heavy eyes, too much to
pay no mind blare don't you dare, a sister's
word-pauses they say don't you dare. But what's the
point of survival in which the recovered one
still prowls and haunts the stake?
I've been trying to wear love on my chest
and say it with my chest, but all roads are
good roads that lead far from this. If I stay here,
this place is going to kill me. And life:
I'm on my ninth go around.

Blue Note

In January, I got a tempestuous goldfish, 1/2 out of love, the
scavenging kind, seeking tethering, 1/2 out of wanting to see
which of us would outlast the other. I said: I am ready.

The sea & her constituents, she always tests me,
brings hope out of me with delicate, many-fingered hands. And
for a tick, I am one with every strident note of my soul: yes

fabled witch yes werewolf yes illustrious thief, yes:
I have lit a match, this match has lit me. If I can take
on the world time and again, what is a webbed challenge?

And yet I know about the pucker, and the disappointment
that always follows, know forty-six different ways
to crack the surface of a heart. Always, I am ready.

The goldfish's leaving was a proof and a taunt.
How does anyone own anything, in this day and age?
How does anyone own and owe oneself?

Blue note, pink cloud, grey sky, pyrrhic victory;
misery strips itself of any and all reward, and I have
taken it on, time and again—what is a webbed challenge?

In other words I wasn't born from yesterday's rain, to be
suddenly wanting the world to cradle me tender. This
many-fingered kind of love, it does not balance, does not

fortify. I've figured I do better where my body slips and sinks.
1/2 out of love, 1/2 out of wanting to see is no way to
live a life: already knew that then. But I just want

there to be still the briny twang of black Moroccan
olives to distract a joyless mouth, dry rice bowls
in which restless fingers comb through rest, steel

guitar strings that whine when you brush them,
the lull of Aznavour on a rainy day, a story worn out
between flicking tome pages, lush embrace of

mother's incense powder. Not much, not much I'm
asking for. I am ready. I want Prometheus to feature
in my lines and dreams, want him to lend me some of

his prowess, dig up from me the fire and give it back
to me mended, restorative. I am ready. I want to be
near good things, near quiet things, I want to be near

the water. The gaping lonely will never go away. I
already knew that then, won't start to unlearn this
now. Maybe next time the goldfish could be a person.

Maybe next time it will be full love, and full
wanting to see. Maybe next time I will take on the world,
and say yes, I am ready, and think and think and mean it.

III. I HOPE MY HEART FOLLOWS

Roundabout Alchemy

A spore of incense ash floats in through the window
from incense holders lining the paradise garden;
a world asleep.
I clasp my hand around the burnished smell.

The slant of the world is different here,
Nouakchott sheathed in silky slumber.
The desert,
it strips you down to
pure moonlit bareness,
til only twilight meanings
and crepuscular truths
make sense.

The sun becomes a pendulum;
the dullness in your chest a percussion;
patience a wrinkle in time's coat;
your bones' ache an atlas to finger your existence.
The buzzing fly's an omen
—you flinch—
that brings mesmeric doom;
the curled toes a grave you dig your family.
For years I thought I killed my grandparents;
black spot on tongue an augury,
words a weapon.
Even sleep means something else here,
bargain made with the cosmos
provided that in daylight your eyes stay
openwideopen:

and spores of incense ash are footnotes to something
monumental,
a revelation,
significance,
creation in slow motion.

I scan the night with milky eyes
privy only to the art that glistens in obscurity,
my aquamarine lungs,
and the lines that make me.

I press into my face and smell
the sweetness from my hands.
Henna squeezed from shorn pouch made
the sweetness from my hands.
Swirls and shapes deposited
into sweetness, in my hands.
The earthy, vaginal smell of it,
sweetness, sweetness hands.

For weeks after, I will walk into every room with palms extended,
offering the beauty therein to anyone;
the gazes I capture, I close my fingers around.
I am trying to say something.
I am trying to say something.
I am trying to say.
Something.
This wouldn't be the first time.

I go back to sleep with burnished smell, significance, creation in slow motion,
cradled sweetly in my hand.

When Sound Came to the Movies

That is what it must have felt like
the experience a concussive wave;
for many, a thrill and then some,
for others a thrill pre-calling trouble;
this cavity inside me it is a panicle
that binds to all other transmutations
of sadness, a sort of hunger-whitenoise,
live wire when touched. *See it, you'll*
believe it, they said. I tried and tried,
crouched against ramparts on dusky days,
trying to pin the bird mid-flight.
At last I entertained the umbral thought,
and the wing, castoff, struck me in the eye,
and the flame went straight for my hand.
The way it comes ashore in you is proof
of the fact: you still don't get it.
A word sets it off and you're left reeling;
saffron-colored sky corners remind you of her
wax print gown. You are cast back there
when whiffs of braised red snappers rip
your restful childhood right out of you.
Although silent, the *Arrival of a Train at La Ciotat,*
would have found me stupefied in my seat, juggling
maddening chasms like: it hurts + it is the truth.
A secret: there is no chasm, never has been.
I hope this serves in any way.
I hope someone else displaced
like me can read into this and say
                    yes, that, exactly that feeling.
Had I asked her, before she died, she'd have said:

> *Think about the universe.*
> *Think of all the ways in which*
> *it has tried to make you see yourself.*
> *How dare you turn your back from it*
> *try to dim its sound,*
> *and call it cruel?*

69

to the white woman who grabbed my head when i was six so she could count my cornrows

first of all, that head yank hurt
bothered a torticolis i'd been nursing
for days
having spent them curved in painful pliés and arabesques

reader, imagine this:
you sit in the empty corridor of a piano recital hall
you wait for your friend to take her turn.
you sit erect, music tinkling from each room illustrating
you, even now, your own incompetence.
you sit wallflower-esque so as not to stand apart (Black girl in lily-white space,
where every
passing eye skewers
you with intentional scorn); so that when this one lingers,
you brace against the coming criticism.
she doubles back.
squawks in shock.

my what a work of art.

and with a manicured claw,
goes to town on her prey,
your head.

woman, you are one of many
some nicer others not so nice
one asks mid-interview if my hair is real
another tugs it while we stand in line
talking about

i can't help myself it looked so soft
some's auras do all the stroking, eyes agog lips parted in voracity
so that's what it feels like
lady takes a fistful of braids in the elevator thinking i won't mind
fingers rake up my scalp as i bend over the cinema restroom sink
looks like lamb skin
scissors slyly passed through the tips of it by a schoolmate sampling my texture

don't you know?

these box braids these passion twists they don't come, don't go cheap
take artful care
hug close to scalp
sometimes, no always hurt
i was taught that to tick off beautiful things without a *mashallah* attracts the
illest of luck

i think of doing then what i always do now
brisk snap up of the wrist
to clasp the offending hand
so hard it would make a snapping twig proud

don't you know
it takes witchery to give it sacred life
each strand its own language
a lacquered song
powdered, varnished like a prayer
i was taught that to touch one's hair is tantamount to communion

i didn't yet know no
that i could say and mean and warrant it
no, no nope, don't think so
fuck no

don't you know
a Black woman's hair is zoetic
to touch Her is to make us adulterers
first lover we resent
last friend we try to make
i was taught that to allow the trespass is to allow faithlessness itself

but above all, you were one of manymanymany
pale hungry hands on my 1B kanekalon-ed, marley twist-ed natural-kinky,
afro-ed, hot-combed,
big-chopped, bantu-knotted, all the works hair
eager eyes concealing contempt
candied tone belying superiority
grit-teethed envy
fetishizing lazer glare

too too big for six year old consciousness
to comprehend
you are all the same to me
and to you, i am surely but a face
and yet i still remember how you taught me
that autumn day in a hostile recital hall
that if it looked intricate enough
hell, even if it didn't
my hair, and its addendum-ed body
was license to touch, to grab, to feel
to own

In Slow Burn Fashion

We had three good months but fires too seldom tended to As the saying goes take to running out It burned your skin and you pretended that it didn't It burned me too You took it well if not stoically but later it devastated you in waves I pretended not to take at all And it came back with a vengeance At the time you were sober much less gone behind the eyes I picture you fingering a guitar you cannot play Pretending you're not humoring the joke of alcoholism bubbled budding like water petals on your lips The sugar hazel of your eyes colored by the stain the saddest blue I think by the time I met you I already knew how to do this How to lose a friend and pretend they left you How to lose a person a country a body a life and pretend they left you I took one look and I said I'm gonna lose this man and do it gladly These days the singeing grinding copper fist it digs a cupola in my chest every-time And I think yes yes this is good This is better than the decade-long pretending Because regret it has brought me to my knees Matthew Not the impish kind that made me leave a city for anothernothernothernother The disorienting kind The humbling kind The kind that makes you consider hands going waitaminutewaitaminutenowwaitaminute Just Wait Until you get it really get it But I've said this already 1/2 out of love 1/2 just for the heck of it is no way to live a life

Creation, Reverse-Engineered

I said I'd tell you about it later, so here it is:

i.
Today I broke my grandmother's mirror and was leveled by the shame of contradictions:
a- the instinct to make of yet another jagged edge my muse, and b- that jagged edge
belonging to my universe woman. I balanced the shard and felt the imminent pleasurepain
before the grief of having splintered the object with which she held her monumental
stare. Only I could blaspheme a memory with the greedy fitfulness of my blood—

ii.
                    no
              let's do this again
           my late grandmother's mirror
            it sits in a white and green
                 square of cloth
             where does a soul go
                 if not in the
            receptacle toward which
            it was always orientated
             I ground in it my knee
           glass into powdered void
               I ate that dust
           fingerpads flicked into it
            and swallowed it whole
               the spare shards
            I tucked in the pocket
            I made against my chest
         each coagulation reminding me
              that it, and by proxy
              she are perennial
                 and also
               the tears shed

when I broke it for her
they were because it must
have hurt her
it hurt me
too

iii.

No. Striking though it sounds, that is a lie.
How about: you were trying to see what you looked like inside/out, and
cutting yourself is a form of philosophy, a perdition exercise, erratic therapy, a
Self discovered in the cleanest articulation,
a raw flesh-to-the-mettle-of-your-reason study in purgatory, a …

iv.
No. Plainspeak this time.

Like pulling honeycombs apart. Convincing myself that things are not things:
inverse artistry. Does not invite interpretation; it divorces meaning from its
source. This madness it takes work, and it pays. It calls on the numbing; calls
on the sedations. Like that time grief was used as a reason for walking off a
stage mid-concert. Like that time I mourned a relapse by rampaging, on a roll,
through willing bodies. Like that time heartbroken I cradled an honest *see
you around*, in my palms, knowing full-well I wouldn't, in fact, be seeing him
again. There is no trick of the light. There is no explanation in that deciding.
I swallowed the shard of my grandmother's mirror so that it could shred my
insides up. So that I could spritz like an artful blood geyser. I just wanted to see
something happen. Could never resist a lively fraying.

ask again tomorrow, america

i'd marry myself before i married you,
& that's a cold-sober claim considering
i wouldn't touch myself with a hundred
foot pole. i don't know what you are
hoping to catch, & friend, i like
your ardor, but. pump those brakes. don't
ogle promises you don't intend to score.
oh, no mistake about it: i double take-d at
your dedication, kept admirable time
with the complex rhythm in your salesman
pitch, made all side-eyes at the way
your brass-tacks, razzle-dazzle, sunshine-
opal mind works. but also: i noticed
while you were cantillating down at me, how
perfect, how like embroidered clouds your
teeth were, & your skin too, cream-blond,
& lacteous. it might not have been fair,
might not have even been on point,
but i called it right away. *this one spends*
too much time on himself, plausibly
not enough on others, & i need less of
that in my life. pardieu, pardieu, i've seen
too much. you say you want what you can't have
as if you don't pluck every thing your flying
eyes alight upon on. my people's lineage is
the proof. if you, the greenhorn, then i,
preceptor, trying to impart what dramatic
irony feels like when lands the punchline

Seafarer Fresque

1.
Not the first, certainly not the last;
Sometimes obliquely
                    (you kind of have an accent),
most times, much more blunt:
                    so where do you come from? Like

                                        really,
                                        really,
                                        really,
                                        really,
                                        really,
                                        really,
                                        really,
                                come from?

2.
there is often a moment after I wake
                when I know not
                            where I am
a second only   maybe two
                quarter rest
the folds in my thoughts smooth themselves out
take in the surroundings/lighting/structure
of the room
I think   could be anywhere
                second more
all prospects rifled through
then it floods me
        and I remember
                and I sigh

3.
I was born in a suitcase on the Atlantic Ocean
Wrapped with tarot cards in silk leaves and cascaded up
Along the beryl waves while my gills molted off
My skin. The waxy briny scent of it a resurrected
Muscle memory

Half myth under duress
The neutral side of pleasant

4.
Nevermind
how many
times I
scram, I
come back
cavalier,
say: *how*
are you so
sure? You
don't know:
I could

      I could

I could

      I could, yes,

I could
belong here.

5.
Deflection: I know that auntie well. *She* wouldn't know
I haven't told her a single thing about myself.

Like that I come from everywhere, and nowhere,
And questions invite disclaimers and clarifications.

Like that I cohere the way one does at a friend's:
Never too cozily, and never for too long.

Like that reinvention is a godsend, these sails have
Saved my life. And houses, not homes, are stopovers.

Like that I measure relations by how likely they are
To survive the strain my of hopping in/out of them

Like that caring about things + places is a heavy
Currency, and it better be damn worth the expense.

6.
There is never a moment, when I don't know
where I am

a museum,
a display from
various golden stays
sparkled playthings that were
                                        never really toys.

I could kill for the generational memoirs overrunning unswept attics
I could slaughter for those heights notched by vibrant pens on kitchen walls

7.
it's christmas and you have narrowly missed your connecting flight home // the
next one // another couple of hours // duration loses context // you drift down
Heathrow like a shade // docking in one spot half a moment // migrating to an
empty terminal a next // novels rifled through in corner bookstore // forehead
pressed on gelid glass panes // careful maneuvering of planes outside // phone
connects-disconnects on the airport wifi // bleary eye contact with stranded
others // laptop discharges somewhere in the sixth hour // breaststroke between
time zones // people flooding gates // others board // a Paddington cutout baits
the buzzing children // lean on the seat back // listen // miscellaneous languages
flitter about // lullaby you half to sleep // like always brain starts its palpating
// you pick up what you can // feel for what you can't // comparing with what
you can // the slow whiling away // perhaps // has made you sentimental //
because it occurs // maybe this is home // liminal space you have always known
// seeing as tangible // it certainly is not // neither garden nor house // nor land
to build upon // maybe home is the green tea you like to drink // maybe it's
the body of water you always look for // maybe it's wherever there is music //
maybe an airport // where you don't have to choose // don't have to commit //
to any thing + one // maybe this ambiguity is good enough // you contemplate
this // rolling luggage wheels // intermingling accents // slap-slap shoes on
polished floor backdrop // and for a juncture second // you almost believe it

Night Work

My baby sister uses Am—*here, take this* in Wolof—
to say both *here you go* and *give me that.*
I become the skittish interpreter

                                                    Am! Am!

inferring each mutable context.
Rattle my insides and French tumbles in
my ear soup. *Take this* and *give me* metamorphose

                                                    Âme! Âme!

There's divinity in her
staunchness, her curt entreaties

                                                    Soul! Soul!

There's divine pleasure in
mastering the world through her
improvised language. She considers
the words in her plump little fist,

then flings them away like joyful noise.

A couple more years, and I could have been her mother
I thank God that I was not. How can I hear what she
does when my ears are sewn shut, blind-hem stitched,
tighter than a drum? Give and take, chasm and release,
what makes you happy makes you miserable and whatnot.
She understands the macrocosm better than I ever did.
It's a wiggling tooth: there's the dull ache of a root
unloosening itself with every jerk, and there's
the joy in jerking it in the first place:

pick your pleasure.

I'd like to make up my own language,
confer twin meanings to words while I strip
that duality from my fellow human souls.

In my hands, language would serenade—

                                        Am! Am!

like she does, and I'd make us all same
and good. A child's wish, yes from a
world-weary, no-longer-a-child.

And I'm lucky I am stubborn.
I have to remind myself,

everyday, that this here shared existence
thing, against all empirical proof,

it is worth it it is worth it it is worth it.
I am discovering in myself a skittish optimist.

This world, it must be good, if only because
it deserves her eyes, her sunshine gaze,
her brain tendrils enveloping it, unbowed.

Yes, dear, I hear you: soul, soul, soul.

the mistress of talking in circles

there's nothing worse than soggy ramen, i replied, and you took it
as evidence of my characteristic flippancy. had you let me finish,
i'd have continued my analogy: there's nothing worse than good things
left to stew, stew, stew until they pickle into ghosts of themselves.

as in: i the soup, you the ramen, i will ruin you if you stay, and all that noise.
there. it's on the nose, not my best metaphor, but one you'd have understood
had you been less angry. once, you called me the mistress of talking in circles
and though i chuckled (*"i have OCD, you bastard"*), it was so as not to wail.

my bad. i've been called punctilious, easily distracted by the minutiae,
chasing tails like bloodsport. you've made yourself dizzy at my flank.
when you told me you were leaving you said *it's for my best* i countered
happy for you, weighing and appraising all the future hurts, hands clasped,

going double file down your marrow for days. another thing you once
told me: i have, sometimes, a mean way of saying things. with a laugh.
sort that makes folk wish they'd never implored me to speak up.
laconic me. these innervations, they rarely get an outlet, so

when they do, mad-dash, slapdash, toes stumbling on toes:
gracelessness downs the apology. i forget the adequate cry,
the suitable words of atonement. i ain't shit. want nothing more than to
plead *i beg you i beg you* and *no*. but i just laugh and laugh instead.

ï

My name is Aïcha with an 'A' and an 'ï' that wears a crown;
non-kin walk all over me and sigh *it's just a name, just*

a name. They desecrate its wilting flower-body
with irregular, secateur-like inflections, sharp and

cutting as the blade of colonial disdain. My name is
Aïcha with an 'A', when you say the word, say it with

your chest. Do not put the offending ʃ after the
the ï. Roll the tongue upward and give that diaeresis some

respect. It's that sibilance that gives flower-body its sway.
You keep wrenching from my hands, and I am back

with my Gorée ancestors, holding tight their names:
Kiné! Leyti! N'deye Fatou! Sarahs and Beths be damned!

I'll look the privilege I have in the eye and say no.
My name is Aïcha with an 'A', I'll let you try that one again.

When people put the tréma on the letter, I fall wildly
to my knees. Sweet mercy, God alive, I'll give you anything

you ask for. When people say, really say my name,
dot-dot-slash and all, I hear: *You, magnificent beast you,*

you take up space and ain't it something, flower-body
cradled in their fingers like the galaxy holds up the world.

I shouldn't have to beg for dignity: it arrived in the palm
of my hand when I was born. It was passed from lips to

lips until the sound was deposited in my father's ear, and he
gave it to me. Aïcha with an 'ï', the crown high on the letter.

(A) Tragedy Mask

'This might be a new way of seeing the world'.
Or no: I'm just the Fool stepping off that
gleeful cliff, with a chin check aimed at
precipices. It was a gaffe at first: now
I'm willfully misplacing my glasses and
testing the day ahead. Do I evade better
when fear is blurred? I am optimistic.
I even tell myself 'see it (not see, sorry)
as a disguise in blessing: hallucinations
gone fuzzy, baobab-carved body gone vague
in reflections. You won't even know where
to start. Every which way you cast glances,
a gouache landscape emerges, softens aversion,
and time has gone molasses'. I even (disregarding
my flesh come tender with collected table
corner bruises) tell myself 'I could get used
to this' and 'what more could I ask for?':

knowing full well that is always the wrong question   i am asking for   even
when i don't know that i am   and that is also the wrong answer   the world
i see may be   all new but my eyes ajar   people read into them the slithering
beasts   prowling making ripples   if it can wait   by god make it wait   i
cannot blame anyone for disbelieving   i look disingenuous   without the
shades to bellify and   cover for them   my masks just don't look the same
and call more furiously to the truth

tell me you're open

i wake from the dream with gashes in my chest
snakes turning warm on my blood
half-interred in the wounds
while i go maybe it was me
surely it was me, surely it was me

athena would have torn
them from me and slung them
at my head to stop the babble
had i, in her temple, done the babbling

it wouldn't have made a difference that i was
sixteen and he thrice that, rapacious
where i was not: he bore poseidon's might
by virtue of being a man. even his
threats colored off like jazzy quips
to surrounding ears

till even i considered
maybe it was me, maybe it was me
till i inflected each word in turn
to change his sentences' meaning

and make them more + less palatable

friendless forlorn empty dysmorphic
and sixteen, and sixteen, and sixteen
the sort of spotlight that should be
exhilarating: gift after
palliation after urging
meant to soft-pedal the panic gong

he said
tell me you're open
instead
don't say no, say maybe
be kind

i am offering love
and you
are killing, are killing
me

violation: to be stripped
to the flaring
flesh, and be demanded modesty

it's been over ten years now
i've said it with less conviction since
knowing better

but sometimes i am capsized
from pre-slumber by that thought
maybe it was me
surely it was me
i said no, said no again
should have maybe sung it like a gorgon

magical negress

it's a misconception that the darkest skin won't bruise or blush or freckle
the realest sleight of hand: though made 'of color', you are in fact color-less
and suffering begets suffering ad nauseam till it burgeons enlightenment
'tell me when your childhood ended' vs 'this wisdom, it takes work, but pays'

but we know what's what. things get harsh-light the longer you stare them down
stardust wings are feet of clay. fear someone will kill me ugly, that i will die hard
if one walks with a fighting foot, one must tussle their way through life
and suffering begets not suffering: ad nauseam, and no burgeoning
enlightenment

i woke up to my days with short fuse in hand and gainsaying, spitfire heart
and why shouldn't i be like a crazy person, why shouldn't i pitch my mast to sea
i'd like to live within means—a pilot's confidence to carry souls to safety
the realest sleight of hand: though made 'of color', you are in fact color-less

'don't tell me when your childhood ended, be the shoulder, the world's mammy'
a misconstruction: the darkest skin bruises blushes freckles bleeds most vividly
i want to open windows when it rains and awe my iridescent scales
i want to say i am doing my best, with my secret voice, and to my one-woman
audience

Essence, Fluorescence

Wayward child of Kaolack and Rosso, where have you been? Broken Wolof
tumbling from your
        lips never matches
the cadences in your head. When you have children, if you have children, that
cadence will
        sound even off-er,
téléphone arabe, grapevine whispers and down and down it will go distorting
itself—what a
        joke—until you
no longer recognize your tribe on your tongue. You didn't pay attention, you
didn't listen to the
        recipes casually
dispensed by your mother at the stove. It's too late for you to pull thought
fragments from
        opaque minds'
eye pools. Even if you whisk your fingers in it and hope, you can only move
forward, you can
        only make mistakes.

Who do you think you are?

Who do you think you are, then?

Say, who do you think you are?

Put a match to your heritage,
see if the fire warms you for a change.

Page-Turning As a Declaration of Love

Because we seldom use our words,
        unmoored and can't relate,

our hands have all the eloquence of
        different languages symphonizing.

The piano is an enclave, we sit at its
        threshold fiddling the waterkeys;

why and when did I leave you? I can't
        keep my eyes off the teeming   surfaces.

You, King Salmon, and I the torrid fishwife;
        I would sell you, but I fear

your high-priced idiosyncrasies.
        And we seldom use our words,

not to wrangle, no longer to haggle.
        When I left you? When you swore

you could not trust me. And yet: when
        I step into bodies of water,

fishes, all in a tizzy, gather around me.
        I read you reading, flick the pages

like my hands belong to you, and I
        know you are the liar: *I don't*

trust you, another myth under half-duress.
        Knowing the floorboards of

a house that groans takes time,
        and in you, you've allowed me

endless wanderings. I may again
    ask for something high-priced,

that says *I love you more than
        love itself*, and carry no shame

to barter it. Don't we both make
        music beautiful again?

                you and your red wine lips

sated on my blood

                you can have my guts and all my

                            salty roe too

A PIPER

At the start, a question,
that turns into a spell
or a mantra, or insanity
you hinge your faith on—
all of it, and then some;

a spell you hope will fail.
You, a babbler, a consummate
fabulist-turned-bullshitter
though you never say a word,
you'd like to know how come

it always happens. Yellowed
sky, burnished landscape,
halting gait, busted navigator,
susceptibility for sucker-
punches: how, how come.

I wonder what the piper felt: rhapsodic? powerful? relishing the carnage?
Or did he go to pieces, imposter-syndrome-like, lonely-in-a-crowd-of-
people-like the longer that line of youthful worshippers got; the more he
realized he'd never have years and years enough to deceive them all?

Because I know and I know
and I know. I'm not the kind
of person others tend to stay
friends with, and the only
story my face will tell is one

in which I frowned a lot and
disagreed too much. I have made
cutting across people into an
art, have made telling people
I don't care in the nicest way

into an art, have made apologizing
and meaning it and not at the

same time into an art. But
ruminations are a misery, and
again, misery strips itself of

any and all reward; yes, though
they cooed and cawed and scraped
my ankles, they were walking so
close, no one asked me what was
wrong. I no longer savor my

composure.

I wonder what the Piper felt, cause I would have told him: devolve in gravity,
I double dare you. Inch that door slowly open. Show me not what raw flesh-
to-the-mettle-of-your-reason you are made of. All that softness you press into
gaping cracks so they do not show, I'm sure your people, they did that too:
dare to try things differently. Whichever way you toss it, however ardent your
worshippers get, you are your own sea, and nobody can sail you but you.

I don't know if I'm a poet;
I don't know if I'm just good with
stringing worlds into musicality—
I don't know if I'm good at even that.
Just that everything else looks

silly between my hands. Haven't
been daughterfriendwomanself
in far too, far too long, I know
and I know, and I know. So I
whistle at the moon, make promises

and I hope my heart follows.
Last to turn up, last to faith,
my fingers too small, dry and twig-like;
still, I hope my heart follows.
I swing my body into the promise
momentum, finger-linked, cross-hearted
soul-wagered love promises, and
hope to God my heart follows.

Retrospect Talk

I've been thinking about your ear.
I've been thinking about all the emails
I never answered/sent. I shape tents with

my knees. When they straighten out, I
make like the drifting bedcovers are pearls
of warm snow. After all my hemhawing, I concede

I may miss your season (winter) again. It's a
paranoia of mine that others can hear my
music. Remember? That thing about conserving

souls inside the songs we listen to?
I would never let a person come that close
again, with unsteady hands to boot.

It's presumption—I'm carrying waterbowls
with buttery palms. Everything I hold
shatters and breaks. And you: have long since

wholesale-d said soul to the first sucker
who came waltzing your way. I am setting
the scene so that you know; because you need

to know, how jarring, how fearful, how terrible
full circles are when you least
expect them. I get it, I get it, remember.

Do you, remember? I was perched on a table
corner, ready as always, to bolt. You,
pontificating: *think of life and people*

as a too-scalding bath. Even if you don't
take in all the way, it's worth it to ease
in, take your time. What did you ever know?

93

When I feel I hate you most, that I could almost
flood the earth you walk on, I think about your ear,
where you kept your soul. In my mind, I finger that

forearm scar, the one you got from shielding
your little brother when you both nearly died
in that car accident. It reminds me:

that

you, on occasion,

have a screaming heart

and

I am much less sad

about you.

Did You Ever Turn Up?

December left me in a state in which I floated like
a ghost through everything & mostly, mostly slept.

& when I did not sleep I thrust the pit of my pupil
at the waltzing hours (look at those dingdongs roam)

& asked Compromise, compromise for what? Except I
wish I were, like Kitt, jeering at the notion of love—

not life-living. I thought of Sula's secondhand lonely,
I listened to Mann's *Mental Illness*, swallowed

After Laughter, then *The Idler Wheel*, then all the
Sad Girl mixtapes my ears could cope with, going

'that is you don't worry, that is not you, don't worry'.
Wasn't I a busy girl? Every month had come with its

excellent line of reasoning: in January I couldn't
stomach another borderless winter. In February, the feel

of my hands on my body pulled me outright out of sleep.
My March birthday was a joke that had long gone over

my head. April & its plainsongs, like a friend who'd
never leave. June & July? Charybdis & Scylla with

their warmth that would sear me: no good. In August I
kept breaking things & on all fours, dustpan & broom

in hand, therein I saw the direst metaphors. Let us not
talk about September. October failed to deliver its

habitual spicy déguisements, preaching instead 'you
need to stop projecting & step into your own life',

& November cast the offense, the unforgivable spell:
a waking story in which I didn't recognize myself

for a moment & felt finally at ease. It was jarringly
foreign. I was going somewhere terminal with this

list, & now find myself asking the waltzing hours
who I used to be before the Storm, before being at the

end of my rope was a state of being, not a transitory
feeling; before the compromise & secondhand lonely

& issues of projection: & the Asking, it gives me pause.
I still don't know what it means, & most days I make

a point not to listen. The months, they have failed me:
again, they have not taken me out, & again I start

the day with a Motives inventory, some stupider, some
deeper-seated: but no go. 'You are out of tricks, woman,

& we are still here', say the hours, except it feels
less a threat, than a long overdue, maybe halcyon

reckoning.

Mouth Noises

When they tore the thorn from Karaba's back,
they saw her agony as fleeting but I knew her

wail for what it was. There was no victory in
her taming, no victory in her joining in the

villagers' chatter. Second-fiddle wildcard, I never
stomached the mouth noises; somehow I feel I

grew up wrong, oblivious to the hearing of the
Call that gathered everyone together, made them

stretch out their hands. People keep thanking me for
being here, disaccustomed as they are from the notion,

and I self-flagellate (why didn't you just do the
niceness you were on the verge of doing? halt when

you walked out the door? risk loving one more time?)
Call me Circe making out of pigs men, and lamenting

her efficacy. I am distressed by the word Community
because neath its velveteen embrace is a frequency

attuned only to a few ears. I hear how the word has
failed others, how it has been tool, firing squad

and appraiser for those who didn't belong. How it
has meant itself and also its reverse. How it

has gated around and against: an alibi, a hypocrisy,
a platitude. My body, again a scapegrace, has not found

itself greeted into the taut spaces the word
chisels out. How does anyone own anything, in this

day and age? How does anyone own and owe oneself, if
even the seawater throws you out, spouting language you

don't yet understand? Telling you *come back when you
are ready for the pinwheeling and the cherries.*

If even your grandmothers and their countries say *no,
wayward child, where have you been?* If even your

Matthews say *we had three months but you came back
too late?* And shattered swallowed mirrors tut-tut *still don't*

get why you're doing this? and the cults you join
with those like you, yearning to whittle away, and

the ghosts who don't recognize you yet, and the past and
future selves who go yes, *I'm going to have a great*

life and you ain't there yet, and pipers and echo-chambers
and essence, fluorescence—they tell what no one

wants to hear. In another century they'd do me like Tituba
and the like. In another century they'd probably say

*look at that bitch, burn that witch and with her all her
joyless fancies. She doesn't know that a good life*

*is with People, and that a crook, or a crocodile
—no, a goddess' temper will sinksinksink her to her seabed.*

Acknowledgements

Acknowledgement is given to the following literary journals and magazines, in which these poems have been published, or are imminently forthcoming.

Ang(st) Zine, "A Little Relaxer"

Birdy Magazine, "ï"

Cephalo Press, "Congratulations! You're In A Cult," "Echo Chamber Sweet-Talk"

The Coachella Review, "my week off"

Doghouse Press, "Bald Eyes," "Apples, Oranges"

DREGINALD, "Lady Macbeth," "unmoor," "to the white woman who grabbed my head when i was six so she could count my cornrows," "Blood Magic," "of tonguesand flames and gratitude"

Electric Moon Magazine, "Pleasure Sounds"

Eunoia Review, "This Would Ruin My Life"

Fahmidan Journal, "magical negress," "when he asks you why you never speak up in group therapy"

FRiGG Magazine, "Retrospect Talk," "Page-Turning As a Declaration of Love," "ON THAT GHOST WE SAW IN THE PARK IN POTOMAC," "When You Let Me Come Up," "Esprit d'Escalier"

Giallo Lit, "Future Self Will Thank You For This," "In Slow Burn Fashion"

Lammergeier, "(A) Tragedy Mask"

Lolwe, "scapegrace," "Essence, Fluorescence"

The Lumiere Review, "phantom crabs"

Luna Luna Magazine, "grapevine gossip," "Hecate's Wheel"

Lunate, "You Were Sleeping So Well," "Tiny Joy," "Anything, Really"

Marías at Sampaguitas, "Trick of the Light"

Mineral Lit, "Blue Note"

Mookychick, "This Is Not a Complicated Memory"

Neologism Poetry Journal, "(It's Because) I'm a Maximalist"

Night Music Journal, "ask again tomorrow, america," "Otherwoman," "Night Work"

Non.Plus Lit, "Never Was Your Color"

Nymphs, "THIS IS MANIA"

PØST, "Mouth Noises," "The Forest, Not The Trees"

Pulp Poets Press, "after a while, all lakes look the same"
PUSSY MAGIC, "Evil Eye," "Roundabout Alchemy"
Soft Punk Magazine, "Did You Ever Turn Up?," "Prenostalgic Aphorisms"
Stone of Madness Press, "A Case Against Your Generous Insistence on Inviting Me to Things"
Tentacular, "sinker"
(Thorn) Literary Magazine, "the mistress of talking in circles," "When Sound Came to the Movies"
Windows Facing Windows Review, "Sidestage"
Writers Resist, "tell me you're open"

Aïcha Martine Thiam is a trilingual and multicultural writer, musician, cinephile and artist, who might have been a kraken in a past life. As a little girl, she fell in love with monstrous mythologies and devastating folk tales, and has been chasing those exhilarating dichotomies ever since. She has made a temporary nest in Salem, MA, but, forever inspired by Hermes and his winged sandals, already has her eye cast toward another distant horizon. Aïcha is an Editor at *Reckoning Press*, co-EIC/Producer/Creative Director of *The Nasiona*, and has been nominated twice for Best of the Net, and The Pushcart Prize; her work was also selected as one of the Best Small Fictions (2021). Her first collection *AT SEA* (CLASH BOOKS), was shortlisted for the 2019 *Kingdoms in the Wild* Poetry Prize. Her fiction, personal essays and pop culture reviews have notably appeared in *The Rumpus, Cosmonauts Avenue, Bright Wall/ Dark Room* and *Screen Queens.* When not dabbling in spooky things, Aïcha chases after bodies of water, tries to befriend hostile cats and curates an ever-growing collection of books, films and musical instruments. Follow her work @Maelllstrom/www.amartine.com.

www.ingramcontent.com/pod-product-compliance
Lightning Source LLC
Chambersburg PA
CBHW021150090426
42740CB00008B/1027